FROM WHERE I STAND: HOW THE SECOND CIVIL(IAN) WAR HAS ALREADY BEGUN

Jeffrey Byrd

CONTENTS

Introduction..IV

Chapter 1..1
Why is citizenship the law of the land?................................1
Fly on the wall...2

Chapter 2..7
The Reagan years: president among presidents........................7

Chapter 3..16
The extremism of white nationalism and the conversion of ordinary law-abiding citizens into race soldiers Super gun owners in America...16

Not Quite The Confederate Soldier Just Yet, But Trust All Of The Pieces Will Be In Place Before The Year 2043

Chapter 4..29
O.J., Obama, and me: a personal history that revealed The racial divide..29

Chapter 5..37
150 million guns in the hands of the 3%. History ignored is history repeated..37
A Lynch Mob of One...43

Chapter 6..46
The true meaning of violence: from a non-violent perspective............46

Chapter 7..54
2043 is coming and nothing can trump that........................54

Chapter 8..60
Reparations now..60

Conclusion..73

Bibliography..75

INTRODUCTION

On May 25, 2020, 17-year-old Darnella Frazier — armed with only a cellphone and the youthful audacity to not put it down — sent shockwaves through America that would reshape the summer and turn attention away from a global pandemic. Darnella's brave actions suggested that she knew what was at stake and — on some deeper level — we as Black people have automatically been conditioned to deal with Black trauma.

What would happen over the next ten minutes would be, what I hope in her young life, her only moment of reckoning with such a harrowing experience as she witnessed and filmed three officers pinning down a handcuffed George Floyd. One applied deadly force with his knee on Mr. Floyd's neck, two others kneeled on his back and legs for the better part of nine minutes. Another officer essentially cleared space for the figurative lynching by threatening pepper spray to anyone who came near[1]. I was on leave at the moment, but I was reminded of the insensitivity and complicities that lied in the responses of my coworkers every time a Black body had been rendered lifeless after an encounter with police. I had always heard the same response. "Why didn't they just comply?" Or, on the other hand, coworkers told me that they needed to see all the facts or even that, after seeing all of the evidence, they felt like it may have been the case of one bad apple. I would see the disconnect in their eyes, and it was like I had to relive the violent account through the conversation and the distant gazes that they offered. It was as if those who had been murdered were not human at all. It was slowly becoming apparent that this was an extension of the violence that we had been witnessing on our televisions. This too was violence, and more importantly, this was rooted in anti-Blackness. In other words, it was rooted in my anti-existence.

I began writing this book several times, and I stopped because I wondered what I could say that hasn't already been said. What voice could I render to be heard in a sea of scholastic titans that pontificate our experiences with such ease and eloquence? Something inside of me was fighting my demons and failure to do more. Super powers are those that possess immortality in comic books[2], and yet I found myself wishing that — if for one brief moment they had been bestowed upon me — I would eradicate the grip of white supremacy once and for all.

There were never any real job titles that thrilled me as a boy, and the one that I secretly coveted was unrealistic. Nevertheless, my dream never dissipated. The super power would be draped in non-violence, humility, and love. It would possess the ability to turn the hearts of all men away from greed and destruction.

We are not merely polarized as a nation. We are segregated by past government policy. We cannot continue to simply address our history from a narrative that simply refuses to explain how we got here in the first place. We have been inviting the most racist elements in this country into our daily politics since the post-reconstruction era, and we have been calling it business as usual. We have been putting a dress on a pig and calling that democracy. We simply have not dared to call it out.

It was Andrew Johnson in the 1860s; it was Woodrow Wilson in the 1900s. It was Nixon in the 60s, Reagan in the 80s, and Trump in the modern era. We have todo more than simply hold racism accountable at the ballot box[3]. Plainly stated, it is not enough to myopically look at things from a one-off perspective. When we witness an insurrection, we should note that we are not better than this, but that this is historically who we are as a nation. To make matters worse, the mindset of most white people is that of a violent nature – by way of indifference and complicitness – which lays the foundation for more demonstrable acts which will culminate to a point of a second civil(ian) war. As such, here is my take on the state of the country.

CHAPTER 1:

WHY IS CITIZENSHIP THE LAW OF THE LAND?

Growing up, I used to think that the sun rose in New York and set in California. Well, honestly, I thought it rose in West Texas and set in East Texas because I had never been anywhere outside of my home state. Texas was my world, and I had no reason to venture to any other place. I was just fine seeing the world through the lens of my TV – all from the comfort of our sofa. However, what became increasingly clear was that the world was just fine with that. I was miseducated and indoctrinated to believe, as taught in my Texas history classes, that Santa Anna was the antagonist and those brave men defending the Alamo were the good guys [4].

Here is the historical truth: Santa Anna was an abolitionist – and those determined to hold down the fort were fighting to preserve the institution of slavery. One of the primary reasons for writing this book was to document my journey as an autodidact and to parcel out my feelings of fear, anger, and oftentimes rage towards an unfair system of the advantage granted to some and denied to others.

I honestly believe that my refusal to vacillate in my pursuit of truth has led me to a deeper understanding of history and a consciousness that is now awakened. I now have the power to release much of that angst by allowing myself to reach out in love and share this experience with you: the reader. Before I invite you on this journey, I must warn you that there is no illusion of a happy ending, and there is no white knight that slays a dragon and saves the princess.

Indeed, this book is quite the opposite. If nothing else, it's a sobering tale of the history of a nation as I see it: in peril. I have traveled and attempted to gain a foothold in a portion of soil that would grant me some semblance of citizenship, largely because I never have felt a true sense of home here. For African Americans like myself, ties to the global citizenry are sometimes all we've had to bear witness tour existence here in America.

Fly on the wall

Oftentimes overlooked. Oftentimes a nuisance. Generally invisible if quietly still. The life expectancy of the average fly is roughly 15 to 30 days — depending on the fly and its environment [5]. I may be a man, but within the breadth of time and the overwhelming context of mortality, in some respects, I am but a fly. And so perhaps the best way to share this story is from that of a fly on the wall.

I learned at an early age that, in America, the esteemed title of ＿citizen 'had historically been reserved for white male landowners before the term encompassed more of the residents at large. But – specifically in a land where we have been historically locked out and commonly denied – I am faced with the haunting question: —Is it worth it?

At times I have found that my footing seemed so unsure when weighed against the tempestuous history of inequality that America has doled out. The thought of the Tulsa riots [6], Rosewood riots [7], and Atlanta riots [8] accompanied me every single time I was confronted with the prospect of land ownership. Though at every closing, I knew I had jumped through every hoop to prevent a breach in class or caste, I remained uneasy. I knew things could easily be taken away in America, and there is a certain paranoia of being Black in America.

Even when not confronted with a firsthand account of overt racism, I realized that I still had to rely on being in a state of perpetual apprehension to survive.

Thus, the issue of trust has always been solely my cross to bear.

White supremacy is the bedrock of our society and must be squarely addressed if we are ever to exist as a singular society. White supremacy predates the forming of this nation and thus inherently predates all of our country's institutions. While speaking to my experiences throughout my 30-year career as a minority in predominantly white work environments, I hope to reveal the violent – but often unspoken – the intent behind the narrative of whiteness. It's this violent intent that threatens our pursuit of a multicultural and democratic society, and it's this intent that prohibits the conversations about reparations of which society is deeply avoidant.

I want to reveal to what lengths the United States of America will go to protect its systems of inequality, and I believe honest dialogue will reveal how intricately woven capitalism is within the systems of inequality to which we have become so accustomed. I will acknowledge some historical accounts about great men, but I feel it is also my job to present their lives in a micro-historical context. I prefer to write about less commonly known facts, as it strips away the romanticism associated with the myths of their personas. I believe it also helps tell a more complete and honest tale. Throughout my life, I have tried my best not to mince words. I have always believed in calling a duck a duck, a spade, and a hypocrite a – well, you get the gist.

Many people would find my views concerning capitalism downright offensive. And many would dare to say that the term —predatory should not precede such a glorious and sacred term as —capitalism. Perhaps they would even tell me that I am a beneficiary of the term and thus am not preyed upon. However, I have never read in a history book or witnessed throughout my life capitalism being practiced without leaving remnants of oppression in its wake. Western expansion, slavery, Jim Crow, the prison industrial complex [9], and extreme financial inequality all serve as examples of such.

When I was much younger, I thought that God created me – as well as those who look like me – as Black. Naively, I thought it was that simple. I was unaware at the time that God was also responsible for biology, and it was a man who unjustly defined Blackness. Eventually, I realized that this was a centuries-old system created to determine who was deserving of access to resources – as well as who should be denied access to those resources. The whole system was a product of what Reverend William J. Barber II calls —bad biology. Meanwhile, the social construct of white supremacy is —sick psychology, according to Rev. Barber II [10].

CHAPTER 2

THE REAGAN YEARS: PRESIDENT AMONG PRESIDENTS

—You start out in 1954 by saying, "N*gger, n*gger, n*gger." By 1968 you can't say "n*gger"—that hurts you, backfires. So you say stuff like, uh, forced busing, states' rights, and all that stuff, and you're getting so abstract. Now, you're talking about cutting taxes, and all these things you're talking about are totally economic things and a byproduct of them is, blacks get hurt worse than whites... And subconsciously maybe that is part of it... I'm not saying that. GOP consultant Lee Atwater in a 1981 conversation that was released posthumously.

Lee Atwater was Ronald Reagan's Chief Political Strategist, so it's no coincidence that this rhetoric and sentiment shared similar context to the policies carried out during the Reagan Administration. However, it wasn't until 2019 that racist comments from a conversation between Ronald Reagan and then-president Nixon surfaced, with Reagan referring to African delegates as —those monkeys and claiming that said delegates were —still uncomfortable wearing shoes [11].

This is from —The Great Communicator? One of the —greatest presidents ever? I would be remiss if I didn't point out the immense white male privilege here, particularly because this interaction had been redacted from the record in order to preserve Reagan's legacy while alive. Reagan isn't the only man who has been afforded such great privilege; in fact, it has largely been a privilege of the great men who came before him who were also regarded in high esteem. They were all given a pass from scrutiny while alive, only to be exposed after death. This is but one example of America's need to erect a hero through a mythological lens of omissions, oversights, and ahistorical viewpoints. It is a tragedy – and even laughable at times – the mundane level of shelter provided by our media to protect this office of pinnacled achievement and the men who have occupied it. It's all part of the myth that America must perpetuate in order to continue to be great. Or rather, to continue to *feel* great.

It is documented that at least twelve of our country's presidents have owned slaves [12]. How do we grapple with the legacy that our country sanctioned these crimes against humanity and allowed for such an institution to exist?

George Washington, our very first president, was revered for his bravery – but even more so for his rejection of the idea of being made king. Additionally, it was said that Washington was one of the wealthiest men during the founding of the nation. However, the fact that he owned slaves suggests that though enslavement was lawful – Washington's actions were improprieties. At some point in time, this reality should have caused an internal struggle with his own humanity instead of continuing to oversee the plunder of other human beings. In present-day America, George Washington would be brought up on charges of crimes against humanity, but in his era that was not the case.

Thomas Jefferson – most notable for helping pen the Declaration of Independence – has a well-known and revisionist account of an alleged affair with one of his slaves: Sally Hemings. Despite his actions, he was never widely accused of any wrongdoing or indiscretion during his lifetime or for centuries after. But let me make it very clear: Thomas Jefferson was neither exceptional nor was he exculpable from his crimes[13]. This is particularly true for the crime of rape.

It was commonplace at the time for slave owners

to defile their female captives, both for pleasure and for increase. One should not wonder why, at this point in history, the number of slaves increased – despite the Atlantic Slave Trade ending in 1808. Revisionists will tell you that these encounters were consensual. However, these slave owners often remained married and enjoyed the fruits of plunder amidst their purposeful destruction of Black family life. The offspring of these encounters were born into a life as rightful heirs of enslavement.

While adored in the public eye, it would later be revealed through several biographies that Thomas Jefferson was actually a horrible businessman and, despite having virtually no labor costs as a slaveholder, he actually died in debt. The only thing of value that was found to cover his debt? The enslaved people of his Monticello estate.

Here we see that the history of separating and parceling out families is as old as this country itself. Similarly, the historical practice of hero worship is as old as our nation as well. These practices not only protect our heroes, but they also protect America's symbols of exceptionalism as justification for white supremacy.

Let's take things back to Reagan. What would almost

certainly spell political doom for most – like his handling of the Iran-Contra scandal, coupled with his war on drugs – were just a few of his tarnished policies that would have forced him to tread close to impeachment if tested with proper scrutiny. However, through a conservative coalition-driven media lens, America chose to spin his entire career by rewarding Reagan with false accolades of singlehandedly ending the Cold War with his firm militarism talk abroad and his —Awe, shucks appeal. What, in present-day, Donald Trump had to accomplish with vulgar language, Ronald Reagan was able to accomplish with a wink and a nod – all the while inciting a class warfare attack on the poor[14].

I wish to point out that even Reagan could not escape the landscape of racial bigotry that not only shaped him, but erroneously catapulted him into the limelight asa public darling. It is not enough to blame Trump for his views on race and poverty in America, because Reagan shared the same views. In fact, Reagan began the use of tax cuts to create the enormous wealth gap that has grown exponentially since the1980s – and that we continue to see today.

We live in a system that is designed to reproduce racial disparities, and we have a history of constant and intentional reproduction through improved mechanisms that perpetuate white supremacy. It is my assertion that the Reagan era was an experiment in a lighter and more tactical version of the current version white supremacy. Immigrant groups were allowed to come over and —become white, which only could occur as a result of the system of anti-Black racism [15]. The coded language of labeling then expanded to coded self-identity language through symbolism and universalism.

In a sense, there was a sort of self-detachment in order to sacrifice for the greater good; this identity would only appear at crucial times when solidarity was actually needed to reinforce white privilege or dominance. When the Reagan rhetoric was unraveling and the —Awe, shucks cloak was exposed, America was able to usher Reagan out of office unscathed – only to surrender his post to his successor: George Bush.

Bush, in order to carry this torch, offered a different spin on this notoriously crafted language. He referred to this phase as a —kinder, gentler nation [16]. Nevertheless, I digress. The context of this should remain on the culture of Reagan: the man who was able to deliver the script and ideology without the slightest hint of nefarious motives.

I remember the summer of 1982. The heat was brutal, there were five of our mouths to feed, and my parents both had experienced brief stints of unemployment that year. My parents were generous people, and it was not uncommon for them to welcome my cousins and extended family members to stay for a brief or extended visit if they happened upon Fort Worth. It was that year, 1982, that I watched my mother break down into uncontrollable tears at the kitchen table.

She was a proud woman, so I'm not sure anyone had ever witnessed this level of vulnerability. While I can't definitively speak to experiences besides my own, I can say that when a mother cries visibly, children typically follow suit. In this case, it was my brother, my sister, and myself crying along, because we knew deep within that it was time to worry. My mother was having a nervous breakdown, as was the case for far too many mothers across America — especially Black moms.

My mother was feeling the effects of the harsh austerity of politics of the Reagan era budget cuts — better known as Reaganomics. I knew that our family was facing financial adversity, but I had no idea to what extent at the time. My siblings and I simply wanted her to feel better.

It was a year of making do. That meant hand-me-downs and ridicule at school, which put me in a place I'd never been before. I wanted to fight the world, and I needed a punchline for this cruel joke that I was blindsided by. Simply put: I needed someone to blame. I am almost sure now and for certain that there was a trickledown effect from the presidency down, all the way down to the tears that landed on the table the day I saw my mom weeping at the kitchen table.

Every single year, Christmas was a time of excitement, abound with gifts surrounding the tree. And when I say every single year, I mean *every* single year —until this one. Sure, a fresh tree went up and decorations adorned it just as they had all of the years prior. But, while in years prior, presents would slowly appear under the adorned tree in the weeks leading up to the big day, that festive sight remained elusive this Christmas.
Some part of me hoped that there would be a flood of presents to appear on Christmas Eve. Unfortunately, that wasn't the case. It was

confirmation that my family was truly experiencing hard times, and I remember thinking I could somehow just sleep this Christmas away into a distant memory. However — much like my dream of presents ending up under the tree on Christmas Eve — that wasn't the case either. Instead, we rose early on Christmas morning and went to the adorned tree only to find three cards. Within those cards were promises of delayed gifts for all. My heart hurt for my mother that day, because having the power to give on Christmas meant so much to her. Always curious, I peeked over to observe the expression on her face as we read the cards; I wanted to make sure that she was okay. There was no expression in her face however, which revealed to me that she had deliberated on this decision for quite some time and had prepared herself for this moment. That morning, we were all solemn — but we still had gratitude for family and the gift of Christmas itself. To be frank, the year of 1982 was one of
introspection, and I truly learned the value of love and family that Christmas Day.

CHAPTER 3

THE EXTREMISM OF WHITE NATIONALISM AND THE CONVERSION OF ORDINARY LAW-ABIDING CITIZENS INTO RACE SOLDIERS: SUPER GUN OWNERS IN AMERICA

Myth #1: There is something exceptional about American exceptionalism[17].

Reality #1: When Americans proclaim, they are exceptional and indispensable, they are simply the latest nation in a long line of nations to make this claim. Among great powers, thinking you're special is the norm — not the exception.

Myth #2: The individualism-dominant belief that human behavior is the result of free choices made by autonomous actors, rather than external forces shaping one's path of achievement [18].

Reality #2: I would often find myself hearing these tropes each day. While they are convenient detractors from things like racial group identity, they never quite seem to l and with the intention upon which they were espoused. They are subtle and common expressions, but they still point to something more nefarious within the white male psyche: the refusal to publicly announce one's tie to whiteness as a power or advantage.

America is chock-full of history featuring men who have been praised in the current moment — until it was discovered that they were steeped in corruption, statutes had run out, and/or provisions had been procured to protect their legacy. This is the culmination of ahistorical accounts, omissions, revisionist tales, and mythology upon which we have relied to provide us with a warped sense of nostalgia for a large swath of white America. Though the outcomes and consequences are real, whiteness is a social construct in which time has been temporarily suspended.

The golden era of the 1980s shelved the 1970s term —white guilt [19] and instead used more elusive terms, like —cognitive dissonance and —plausible deniability. A vast number of Americans felt gagged and bound by the revelation of the past transgressions of their forefathers against those deemed as —others yet still supported racist policies that amounted in a stern and zero-sum position requiring the suffering of people of color in order to maintain a so-called racial balance [20].

The stockpiling of guns spurred on by fear — and craftily designed by the stronghold of the NRA — created an environment of mental instability. However, the NRA also realized that it could operate as the most powerful lobbying body protected by the Second Amendment: arguably, for many Americans, the most coveted amendment of all [21]. Ironically, the Second Amendment has strong ties to the First:

the right to free speech. All the while, thanks to a president who was willing to lay it all on the line, many of those within Donald Trump's base are religiously centered within the Second Amendment.

I could easily state that I have worked with many of these Trump supporters, and it wouldn't be much of a stretch to claim that they are the case study for this chapter. These unwitting suspects of a future war finally have a voice in Washington again. All the while, Trump's arrogance, brashness, and even his childish tantrums seem to be lost and largely ignored partially because of what seems to be a larger cause. The looming and impending threat of a non-white majority for the first time in American history — which will likely occur between 2040 and 2050 — creates the perfect storm for angry white men to take back their country and restore it to a level of respectability by way of violence.

I would like to take a more in-depth look at these men, most of whom are blue-collar workers and mid- to highly skilled laborers and subject matter experts. For this population, there are nuanced ways — coupled with a veiled layer of class warfare and the meritocratic belief that if you work hard then you can be part of the upper 10% of society — that advance them in society. Moreover, if you just apply the formula that was laid out before you, you will eventually succeed — generation by generation. The only thing that could possibly disrupt this chain of destiny is social change. This change threatens the very existence of life as it is currently known. In their eyes, the potential for social change threatens the heirloom of inheritance that belongs in the hands of its rightful owners: them.

White nationalism and cognitive dissonance are going to lead the charge into the next civil war [22]. Everyone thought that the conservative strain of dog whistles that was created in the 1960s — and subsequently perfected in the Reagan era — was going to last forever. The big government versus states' rights argument would go undetected with its racial undertones and instead would mask the true, inherently sinister sentiment behind maintaining the status quo.

This anti-government sentiment stems from the 1800s during the Reconstruction period when Lincoln sent troops into the South to ensure that the law of emancipation was followed [23]. Later, during the 1960s, that same effort was utilized when troops were used to integrate the South. During both eras, the summoning of these federal troops was for one particular reason: to halt the terrorization of Black folks. The government is beholden to capitalism and class structure in order to maintain its power and global image. The lynch mobs of yesteryear and the neo-confederate militias of today are and were inextricably tied and beholden to white supremacy and its structural intangibles, as well as white privilege and white identity themselves. Although unwittingly, one thing that the Trump Administration can be applauded for is stepping up efforts to delay the 3% in taking matters into their own hands. For the time being, he gave them a sense that one of their own had infiltrated the Oval Office. For these men, the election of Barack Obama meant the threat of him coming to take their guns. And though it never happened, they stockpiled guns.

Obama was re-elected for another four years, and these men subsequently stockpiled even more guns and assault weapons.

When Donald Trump was elected, instead of relaxing, they still guns. This ever-present display of fear is constantly being masked by a thinly veiled — but clearly fragile — appearance of masculinity. This can be seen even at the blue-collar level, since whiteness represents the power to control the access to and denial of resources. Thus, the act of gathering and hoarding hundreds of millions of guns over the past few years was and still is the average, secular, poor, and middleclass males' contribution to maintaining dominance and securing whiteness as the most visible force in America.

It is arguably the equivalent of putting money in the bank — but not trusting the bank.

The bank, of course, in this analogy is the government and its institutions. Even though your money is generating interest, the cumulative and chronicled adverse outcomes are constantly on display for all to see. Through the mass purchasing of guns and ammunition — leaving others quite literally outgunned and outside of this power structure — these would be soldiers are not leaving anything to chance.

What is also common among most of these capitalist soldiers — other than phenotype, educational attainment, and a firm belief in meritocracy — is the fact that they subconsciously dress and act to emulate white authority. They often buy cars that look like patrol cars, ride Harleys fashioned after police bikes, and they take pride in the uniforms or garb they proudly display in public on the way to and from work. From the security guard to the mechanic, to the police officer, it's all the same.

What typically brings this article of nostalgia to life is the American flag that is sewn onto the garment. This symbol creates its desired effect in the most hypnotizing way. One only has to see the numerous demonstrations by unmasked white folks, armed with high-powered weaponry, paramilitary fatigues, Hawaiian printed shirts, and their boogaloo decree in order to witness this in action as they protest pandemic rules. One will have to wonder if an officer only has to recognize the kinship between the symbol on his sleeve and the larger symbol being waved in front of him to give pause for the cause and allow ill-placed insults to be hurled in every direction —without recourse.

Now, juxtapose this against the protestors of multiracial and ethnic backgrounds protesting police brutality without a stitch of the American flag to be seen. Perhaps this demographic has not put the same level of credence in an object —much less a symbol — that, given its face value, is simply a piece of cloth never meant to represent them. I would be remiss if I didn't mention Fannie Lou Hamer's compelling interview in 1964 where she talks about the American flag being —drenched with our blood [24]. I must also mention a poignant piece of video footage of Black protesters, young and old, during the _60s. They were carrying small flags in an effort to display their desire for citizenship, and police officers did their darndest to rip the flags from the protesters' hands as if to also snatch their humanity away in the process. In the absence of something so coveted it can only be seen as an affront and an assault on the very thing that silently conveys white identity and privilege. It allows the convenience of identity transfer without the hassle of carrying around any guilt.

But just how long can these folks avoid mentioning whiteness when its footprint of privilege is written on every structural artifact and is seen in every institution? There is literally not one inch of this society that was not created to accommodate this specific label. This is the very thing that sandwiches these folks in between a time where it was verbose to claim white identity, and a time in the near future where if you don't claim white identity, you may never get the opportunity to claim it again. To have to bear this reality must be an extremely cumbersome burden right now, given that for the last 40 years or so these people have not had to feel its weight.

I find myself glued to the TV nowadays, not just to witness the latest blunder or gaff by Trump, but to look for clues and signals that might trigger the race soldiers that are hidden in plain view. Unlike presidents of yesteryear that relied on dog whistles, Donald J. Trump has left no doubt in my mind that his mission is to sell white supremacy stripped down to its core.

The community of Trump supporters is indeed a cross-section of Americans across the U.S., and the fact that his approval rating wasn't lower during his presidency should really give reason for concern. So, how did all of this play out at my job? I had all but withdrew all interaction with coworkers who labeled themselves Trump supporters, because I knew that the prospect of engaging in simply one substantive conversation about the things central to my existence would be futile. Even worse, I realized that every conversation would be central to theirs. That was the point when I realized that my time was limited. Every mistake or miscue was heavily scrutinized, and it had become almost impossible to maintain the expected level of perfection needed to stave off the weight of racial judgement and pathology. I would watch as these race soldiers justified Trump's antics on the daily. It is what I had always known and had always seen for the better part of 30 years.

I want to visit the ties that bind the not-so-subtle neo-confederate soldiers and those that straddle the fence as they wait for the right trigger to engage in self-preservation. The fragilities are remarkably the same when you hear the rhetoric firs hand on your job and you can readily pull up an article or publication to confirm how these particular ideas and feelings truly permeate the segregated white neighborhoods across America. When you pair the white nationalists with the everyday white folks who tote guns in these shared neighborhoods, they become dormant terrorist cells of sorts.

The necessary sacrifices of whiteness preservation have oftentimes been exhibited, but arguably more so in recent days. What fear, for example, must one have in order to take their own life in order to protect the amulet of whiteness? I had never really considered the sacrifice of dying in order to deny others access to goods and as a strategy of warfare, but it appears to be a type of mental sickness tied to the notion of not having functioning skin privilege. In her book titled *White Fragility*, Dr. Robin Di Angelo talks about the weaponization of whiteness in threatened spaces as a delicate strategy of warfare. Often operating from a framework of meritocratic belief, white men are easily accepting of the narrative of warrior policing, which appears to deliver them from the burden of guilt that plagues them but would continue to afford them the creature comforts of being white [25].

The conundrum of carrying this burden of guilt, privilege, and the work required to forget such can be cumbersome — especially when confronted with the truth of how they operate. From where I stand, it is not merely the fear of shrinking homogeneous spaces in America, but the fear of losing the power of whiteness itself.

This is evident by the growing number of suicides by gun violence, opioid overdose, healthcare self-neglect, and most recently, the refusal to wear masks. Based upon the data, Blacks are dying at a disproportionately higher rate, which reminds me of the Lee Atwater mantra, —Blacks get hurt worse [26]. These would-be race soldiers are already armed with the greatest weaponry known to man: lack of empathy, indifference, intolerance, and greed.

Not Quite The Confederate Soldier Just Yet, But Trust All Of The Pieces Will Be In Place Before The Year 2043

I predicted that the aforementioned fence-straddlers would convene with the far-right extremists to round out an army of Trumpian soldiers, and I knew that for the first time in our history we would see in real-time one individual selfishly bring the country to the brink of a modern, large-scale insurrection simply to avoid standing trial against the litany of criminal offenses the he amassed while in office.

And indeed, that happened on January 6, 2021. More alarmingly, however, is the fact that insurrection will likely happen on an even greater scale on the road to 2043. Trumpian soldiers will once again quickly turn on the American citizenry if it is deemed — at least in their eyes — that the government is not ultimately working in their best interest. The racist ideology that would lead to a second civil war has a window of opportunity through the political career of Donald Trump, and Trump knows how to stoke the flames of fear in his base [27]. However, I would rather turn my attention to that base. Because rather than refer to them as a possession of his, I would much rather refer to *him* as a possession of *theirs* to maintain the very thing that would last much longer than an 8-year bid in office — regardless of who is officially running the government.

Trump's efforts to accelerate anti-immigration policies, especially during the coronavirus pandemic, will quell by force the racist sentiment and effort to stop the browning of America by the year 2043. The fact that 17 states currently have a higher white death rate than birth rate is an alarming statistic. However, one that could possibly sound off an even more alarming bell is the fact that, between 1999 and 2018, there has been a 35% uptick in white male suicides [28]. By many standards, it is becoming increasingly more difficult to maintain social status distancing without the receipt that comes along with undeserved privilege.

Donald Trump is a prime example of how all it takes is an authoritative figure with a handful of misguided principles to topple a fragile society built on ahistorical accounts. His presidency rivaled that of no other president — save that of the president of the confederate states. Ah, the good ole Jefferson Davis. Alas, Donald Trump's administration was clearly the right administration to commit heinous crimes in the form of domestic terrorism, factual omissions, myths, symbols, and greed. The tonality of the narrative is very critical for Trump as he is a horrible dog whistler. But then again, it shows the level of desperation that an entire party, on the brink of extinction, will resort to in order to maintain the status quo.

This crowd has endured two generations of cognitive dissonance and plausible deniability through a jaded lens of color blindness, all thanks to Ronald Reagan and an era that allowed these generations to shelve their racial identity with a wink and a nod. Whether Trump was trying to invoke the Insurrection Act of 1807 or appeal to his base, it became clear that he was primarily concerned with protecting himself from further personal gain — with moving the country forward remaining the last thing he was concerned about. Let's be clear: the six-time bankruptcy king has made a mockery of the office by manipulating white America's historical xenophobia and racial hatred of others.

CHAPTER 4

O.J., OBAMA, AND ME: A PERSONAL HISTORY THAT REVEALED.

THE RACIAL DIVIDE

Before I begin, it should be noted that I have never met O.J. Simpson or President Barack Obama, but I feel that it is imperative to understand that the actions of each of these men — whether born out of self-interest for one's own gain and self-aggrandizement, or the interest of the millions of Americans that so desperately needed change — the events that encapsulated the apex of their notoriety impacted me in a significant way.

I could get straight to the point by telling you that I've worked with a lot of people who actually believed that Michelle Obama is a man, global warming is just a hoax, the Civil War was a war of northern aggression, and that the South will rise again. The latter has actually been a work in progress since the Civil War.

Whenever there is a social sign of progress, in particular a sign of Black social progress, it was more often than not met with white backlash or austerity politics. Within the workplace, I'd be met with isolation and looks of contempt by work colleagues as a reminder that my very presence represented some sort of breach within this safe haven of mythology. Initially, I would write these sorts of things off as isolated incidents that would randomly occur because of the limited exposure to information back then. To be clear, in the early 1990s we didn't have an abundance of information readily available at our fingertips, nor did we have the sources from which to draw upon as we do now. On March 3, 1991, the traffic stop of a man named Rodney King, which should have at worst, resulted in perhaps a DUI, became a pivotal moment in our history that revealed the decades long, racial tension between the L.A.P.D. and the Black and Brown communities that make up a large portion of its citizenry, [29]. The video footage that was captured told the whole story…....Or so at least we thought. For the first time, America was allowed to see what young Black and brown men had been talking about for decades. Several officers beating an already subdued king with batons — all caught on camera for the first time by an ordinary civilian. This, too, was shaped by an era of colorblind politics and plausible deniability — but most of us did not recognize it as such. And so, it is true that he who controls the narrative control's public opinion.

The Rodney King era was noted for the infamous Rodney King trial.

Interestingly enough, it was called that — and not The Cops That Beat Rodney King On Tape trial, because we all know that's what really happened. Long story short, the cops beat

Mr. King, and they subsequently beat the charges that had been levied against them. I was devastated, because for the first time a lot of people my age, including myself, had never before witnessed the violent and turbulent relationship between the LAPD and the Black and brown communities they patrolled — at least not outside of the exposure we received through West Coast rap lyrics. But here it was caught on tape. The acquittal of this group of officers — by a jury of its all-white peers — incited several riots. These riots would prove to dominate all of the media attention and would soon dwarf the initial story altogether [30]. Like clockwork, the framing of this imagery would result in the recurrent shaping of the narrative of Black violence as pathology — instead of as an act of despair. Whether it was a Black man being corrected through violent means or whether it was him destroying his own neighborhood out of frustration, he simply could not escape this socially constructed assignment.

As tensions began to settle and seemingly heal from this incident, the story of —Juice being on the loose hit the airwaves. It was 1994 and Orenthal James Simpson — better known as O.J. to fans and the general public — was spotted by every network in his infamous white Ford Bronco driving down the freeway with what seemed to be at least a dozen squad cars in pursuit. It was a media bonanza and almost too surreal. As when all heroes go off script, you find yourself grappling with the question, —Why? I only knew of the O.J. that I had grown to admire. I never knew much about his political views or the way that he carried himself in private, but as far as running backs were concerned, he was larger than life and every time I touched a football as a kid, he was the person I emulated.

All of this was hard to digest, and I was forced to separate the man from the image of him that I had created as a young boy. It was time for me to accept the reality that O.J. was possibly more than the main attraction of the famed backfield revered as —The Electric Company, or the handsome face that white America entrusted enough to endorse their products. O.J. just might be a murderer.

I recall the stark contrast between this verdict and that of the King verdict when it came to the interest of my white work colleagues. The latter seemed to draw more ire and scrutiny than the former. Now let's be clear: the loss of life — and two at that — is tragic and horrific. The country found itself in the grips of the irony of the past and the failed policy of modernity that says time heals old divides, which is not the truth.

I vividly recall how long it took me to feel like one of the guys on my job. I told myself that this minority thing was perhaps just circumstance and that I had every right to be here just like everyone else. I can assure you that today I am no longer that naive or eager to be accepted, for the day of the O.J. verdict would be one that would haunt my memories forever. —Not guilty was the verdict, but hell was what I got from my white peers. His victory was sure to be just that: his victory and his alone. —Not guilty sure did feel guilty. Guilty for being unapologetically Black. Guilty for thinking I was equal. Guilty for not thinking I was equal. Guilty for not treading lightly enough. Guilty for not being white. I lost all my work friends that day, and whatever solace that I would find that day had to wait until my shift was over. I was ostracized for simply being. Though over a period of time the resentment of Black bodies in the wrong spaces seemed to drift away and white people began to soften up again, it was just not the same — nor would it ever be the same again.

Barack has been our only Black president. And while I have an immense amount of pride in that, I also feel that the more telling sign lies within who America is. In fact, it is actually more paramount, and could be highlighted by who preceded Barack — as well as by who succeeded him. Barack's identity was sandwiched in between two of what could be considered arguably the worst presidents in modern day history, party affiliation aside [31]. George W. Bush, who was Obama's predecessor, left a legacy marred by a questionable war in Iraq that was centered around a lie based off of weapons of mass destruction and an abysmal economy. Because of the horrible numbers produced in that economy, America — AKA white America

— turned to a candidate of hope and audacity. At least, enough of white America to cross over a racial threshold and usher in a new era in America.

It was an eight-year experiment in American history that saw our first Black president; enter Barack Hussein Obama.

Obama's brilliance, style, leadership, and ability to create the illusion that a divided country was united — despite its refusal to accept its violent past and present — are cumulatively what made this man unique. Like O.J., Obama fed hope to the Black imagination. His playing field was the highest office in the land. O.J. played on a field that for the most part embraced him on Sunday — and if there was any racial hate to be disbursed, he didn't hear it.

He was famous for saying, —I'm not Black, I'm O.J.

Obama had to tune out the hate on a daily basis and also shield his family from the barrage of racial insults and threats hurled at him daily. All of this while tackling key initiatives like turning an economy around, passing an affordable healthcare act, working on Wall Street reform, turning around the auto industry, and passing a Fair Sentencing Act just to name a few. In fact, we could only imagine where this country would be if the term limit was 16 years. But in his book, *We Were Eight Years In Power*, Ta-Nehisi Coates brilliantly reminds us that the only thing that white folks hate worse than bad Black politics is good Black politics [32].

Identity politics is usually discussed when we talk about a gender other than male and when we talk of a race other than white — but perhaps we should look at the summation of all politics as being identity driven. The fact that Obama would have to dissociate himself from his racial identity in order to appease white America could not have been more evident than in the response to his statement, —If I had as on, he'd look like Trayson. America considered that sort of language incredibly divisive and Obama subsequently used more passive language when discussing race going forward. Even with this approach of respectability, there was the notion that, although he held the most esteemed office in the land, Obama had better know his place within the greater context of an already established hierarchy [33].

Another one of Obama's statements that I found problematic is when he quipped, —I'm not the president of Black America. I'm the president of the United States of America-- when asked about addressing issues specific to the Black community. But as African Americans, we understood that this is America, and that this is as central as America would get — at least for us. When Donald Trump preemptively began his campaign on racially inflammatory rhetoric, that was thinly veiled by a nationalist birtherism sentiment, the media somehow avoided labeling it as such. In fact, the media allowed him the courtesy of becoming a central figure in the public eye. Prior to the Republican primary, Trump had no platform other than hate, and America allowed him to publicly and unabashedly display his white privilege. Of course, they did not regard it as such, but what was unfolding was pretty obvious to those of us who are leery of American politics. Regardless of the depth of understanding or the degree of intelligence that each man possessed, White America had the final say in how each of these men would be remembered in the annals of history. While this is not an indictment of either, it should be noted that it is a simple examination of the world in which they were allowed to navigate given the narrow window of public notoriety alongside the constant threat of demonization at every possible misstep.

CHAPTER 5

150 MILLION GUNS IN THE HANDS OF THE 3%. HISTORY IGNORED IS HISTORY REPEATED.

As previously stated, 3% of Americans own 50% of all the personal guns in the United States of America [34]. Additionally, alarming research conducted in 2017 by the Graduate Institute of International and Development Studies revealed that, although Americans made up 4% of the world's population, they owned about 46% of the entire global stock of 857 million civilian firearms. That's roughly 120.5 guns for every 100 residents, and twice as much as Yemen — its nearest rival for distinction at 52.8 guns per 100 residents [35].

A common mantra is that, as Americans, we are a country full of responsible gun owners governed by sound laws that hold everything together for the most part. We always seem to look on the brighter side of things — only to be let down time and time again by a report of a mass shooting. While I cannot claim to have worked with anyone who has purported to carry out such an act of evil intent, I must admit that the level of indifference after each occurrence — in the attitude of those with whom I worked — simply boggled my mind. The only concern was centered around their personal guns, without any regard for the human lives that had just been sacrificed. Perhaps it is because we have collectively avoided confronting this shared indifference and have otherwise conditioned ourselves through an unrealistic lens of hope and optimism that those who penetrate such acts are un-American. The fact of the matter is that, from the conversations that I was not supposed to hear, those shooters are indeed American — and the very idea that somehow, we have magically become a society where modernity has healed old wounds stemming from bad behaviors of the past is a stalwart and convenient distraction. We medicate ourselves into believing that we are better than this at every turn, and we lull ourselves into the belief that if a mass-scale domestic terror attack ever occurred, there are the belief in place to quell an insurrection and restore order. There are still enough citizens armed with intolerance and hatred — beyond the militias and extremist groups — to initiate civil upheaval and disrupt an entire society in order to carry out the task of white genetic survival, and I think it is high time that we discuss this pink elephant in the room. It is not my desire to frighten anyone, but instead to paint a sobering picture from my experience overhearing conversations as an unwelcome outsider. Out of love, I want you to know that I care enough about your wellbeing to not lie about what I think. And as such, I must say that I think there is a mental illness within this country when it comes to protecting white spaces. Truth be told, it hides in plain sight. No offense to the gun aficionados and collectors out there, but these titles have been overly occupied — and perhaps even tarnished — by those that simply revere the power of the gun to neutralize, destroy, and plunder. Even in light of this factor, it is necessary to discuss that it is still unclear just how actively our government is monitoring homegrown white nationalist extremist groups or labeling them domestic terrorist groups. What is clear, however, is that the largest threat to American society since 9/11 has been attacks by white supremacist groups. What has also been clear is that in almost every attack the motive has been to start a second civil war.

If there were ever such groups of color—which, by the way, would automatically make them synonymous with the left — they would have made every news cycle. They would have been thwarted in any and every effort as well, and more importantly there would have been laws passed in order to uproot them as a threat. But these white supremacist groups are often protected by the First Amendment, followed closely by the Second Amendment, and the ugliest and most fortified protection to their credit is American history itself. Not to steal any thunder from the Three Percenters, the Oath Keepers, the new Ku Klux Klan, Wolverine Watchmen, Boogalou Boys, or other white extremist groups and their militia movements, but one can only imagine what accounts of untold history must have been like during the more brutal periods of the late 19th and early 20th century. This time period in America saw almost 5,000 lynchings and the general approval of law enforcement. Some would argue that these acts were intrinsically tied to the cult-like religiosity of white supremacy and because America has not dealt with its racist and violent roots during this era — but instead chose to hide or ignore these egregious crimes against its people — present generations have inherited the lust to return to the indoctrinations of this past. Present Black generations will suffer because of this reality.

In 2016 Northland College sociologist Angela Stroud found that racial anxiety was a significant reason for the uptick in gun purchases. Stroud went through concealed carry applications in Texas and interviewed applicants, and in the process found that many applicants wanted to protect their loved ones during the impending race war [37]. Let me emphasize that once again: *many of them wanted to protect their loved ones*. Having a reasoning like that makes their cause all the more noble, and through plausible deniability allows for the framework of hatred to be taken off the table as a primary reason for amassing guns.

While it is definitely not wise to lump everyone that meets this phenotype intoone group, it is important to thin out such a dangerous group for further dissection.

Members of these organizations tend to be less educated, for example. According to Pew Research, about 26 percent of white people with a bachelor's degree or higher own a gun. Conversely, a much more significant percentage of white people without at least a bachelor's degree — to the tune of 41 percent — own at least one gun.

Meanwhile, for nonwhites, there is no significant difference in the rate of gun ownership in relation to educational attainment [38].

A 2013 study shows that a 1-point increase in the index they used to measure racism increased the chance of gun ownership by an astounding 50 percent. Forman conservative men, the gun feels like a force for order in a chaotic world [39]. Ina series of three experiments, Steven Shepherd and Aaron C. Kay asked hundreds of liberals and conservatives to imagine holding a handgun and found that conservatives felt less risk and greater personal control than their liberal counterparts. This wasn't about familiarity with real-world guns, as gun ownership and experience did not affect Shepherd and Kay's results. Instead, conservative attachment to guns was based entirely on ideology and emotions.

Science Quarterly reported that possessing a firearm actually increases the likelihood of voting Republican. Additionally, this subset of the population is struggling financially: —We found that white men who have experienced economic setbacks or worry about their economic futures are the group of gun owners most attached to their guns says Paul Froese, author of *Gun Culture of Action*.

The aforementioned population is not very religious; the researchers found that religious men often didn't have the same attachment to firearms. Many of that population does happen to be anti-government, however. The researchers noted that gun owners considered themselves to be patriotic, but reasoned that —government was different from the —nation [40]. The thing to focus on here is the hidden meaning behind tropes such as —misgovernment and —states' rights which easily made the 2008 and 2012 election of President Barack Obama the target of transfer. Stroud also discovered another motivation driven by anxiety. —A lot of people talked about how Obama's election was to blame when asked about their reasoning behind the urgency to obtain a concealed carry license: He's for free health care, he's for welfare. "They were asking, whatever happened to hard work?" Obama's presidency, they feared, would empower minorities and threaten the property and families of white people.

What I have found in my experience in being in close quarters and interacting from year to year with some men that consider themselves to be white and Christian, is that many of them fall within the super gun owner category as well. I have also gathered that those within this group purchase guns at an aggressive rate and pass firearms down from generation to generation. Along with such an inheritance comes also the fear of a browning nation. So much for the term, —What would Jesus do? But of course, this would definitely suggest some internal struggle — which not all members of this subset of the population experience.

A Lynch Mob of One

Americans should shudder at the thought of an assault rifle in the hands of a white supremacist just as they shudder at the memory of the lynch mobs of white supremacists. The carnage of yesterday is today — and it seems never ending. Lynch mobs terrorized Americans for nearly 100 years. How long will these new lynch mobs of one terrorize Americans as well?

Moved by the victims of gun violence, antiracists are struggling to ban assault rifles and control the flow of guns, just as they struggled unsuccessfully to ban the lynch mob a century ago. Moved by the National Rifle Association, racists are simultaneously struggling to defend assault rifles, just as they struggled successfully to defend the lunch mob a century ago.

The U.S. House of Representatives passed the Dyer Anti-Lynching Bill in1922, just as in February of 2020, the U.S. House of Representatives passed H.R. 8 to enact universal background checks for all gun purchases [41]. However, filibustering segregationist senators blocked anti-lynching legislation for decades, and, more recently, former

Senate Majority Leader Mitch McConnell chose to block H.R. 8 from receiving a vote despite overwhelming bipartisan support.

No one in Chicago's lynch mobs wrote a manifesto to explain an attack in 1919. If someone had, it would have resembled the manifesto linked to Crusius. —The attack is a response to the Hispanic invasion of Texas. They are the instigators, not me, it said. —I am simply defending my country from cultural and ethnic replacement brought on by an invasion. Swapping out Hispanic for Black and Texas for Chicago, the 1919 manifesto would have read, —*This attack is a response to the Black invasion of Chicago. They are the instigators, not me.* The lynch mob of many and the lynch mob of one are formed of the same racist logic: protect white supremacy. Crusius wrote at length about —losing Texas and a few other states with a heavy Hispanic population to the Democrats, which would allow them —to win nearly every presidential election. Senator Ben —Pitchfork Tillman defended the lynch mob on the floor of the U.S. Senate on March 23, 1900. —*We of the South have never recognized the right of the negro to govern white men, and we never will. We have never believed him to be the equal of the white of t*he of the time, lynch mobs were snatching the political and economic power of African Americans, justifying the carnage by also claiming, —*We will not submit to [the Negro's] lust on our wives and daughters without lynching him*, as Tillman said in the same speech. But as the anti-lynching crusader Ida B. Wells had already written in Southern Horrors: Lynch Law in All Its Phases: —*Nobody in this section of the country believes the old threadbare lie that Negro men rape white women* [42].

The threadbare lie energizing the lynch mob today is that the Latinos are invading, the Muslims are terrorizing, the Jews are exploiting, and the Blacks are infesting. The threadbare lie of Trumpism is that these groups —will hasten the destruction of our country to use the El Paso shooter's words. Instead of viewing these threadbare lies on the big screen through The Birth Of A Nation, which was shown at the White House in 1915, the potential lynch mobs of one are viewing them on the little screen, watching Fox News — just like their former leader in the White House.

CHAPTER 6:

THE TRUE MEANING OF VIOLENCE: FROM A NON-VIOLENT PERSPECTIVE

—Nonviolence means avoiding not only external physical violence but also internal violence of spirit. You not only refuse to shoot a man, but you refuse to hate him."

- Dr. Martin Luther King Jr.

Dr. King is still one of the most important figures to ever exist in America, and I wanted to use his words as a beacon of light to usher in this chapter. I believe that the world, as it was given to us, is too tragic for naive optimism. While I remain hopeful for change, I know it must come from outside of the paradigm of the norm.

There are many wise people who have helped broaden my worldview and seething through a deeper lens. One of the most prophetic voices that I have yet to encounter is that of Reverend Dr. William Barber II, as he carries the baton of justice in resurrecting the poor people's campaign that Dr. King relinquished upon his death on April 4, 1968. Born nearly five years prior to King's assassination, Barber has become the touchstone for what ails America as it continues to mount its capitalist attack on the poor of this country. Barber's dogged pursuit of justice is nothing short of remarkable, and his ability to galvanize people from all walks of life in an effort to eradicate poverty some would even dare to describe as King-like. Additionally, his deep commitment to moral fusion coalitions to bring about change in America is unrivaled.

I have never owned a gun and I have instead always felt that I was protected by a higher power, because I always believed that the pen was mightier than the sword. And though times have become more uncertain during this new era of redemption, I will continue to trust in that higher power. It is Reverend Barber that calms my uneasiness, with his powerful words that insist that my heart is in the right place — although I see the work ahead that should be done in America.

Reverend Barber also reminds us often that if we are to walk upright, then we should be willing to address those things or people in our society that are at the core of injustice. We have a society that often gets in its own way, typically preferring comedic relief over serious matters. This is a purposeful cultural avoidance to deal with the larger issues that plague us. This is a process of normalization that breaks down the fabric of principles and morality that are said to have been the pillars of this nation.

There is no better example of this then when we see Saturday Night Live's interpretation of Mitch McConnell being portrayed in costume as the grim reaper.

While it makes his presence more palatable, it does nothing to ease the suffering and mayhem brought about from his obstructionist behavior that prevents substantive progressive policy.

McConnell's coming of age appeared just as the era of Dixiecrats came to amend. And keep in mind: the Republican party has organized its entire electoral strategy around the dismantling of civil rights. Granted, the same folks that were once the Dixiecrats soon became the Republican party as we now know it — as Lyndon B. Johnson apparently predicted when he signed the Voting Rights Act and the Civil Rights Act. The Democratic party had lost the South for good, and the South and the majority of white people have voted Republican since 1964[43].

What the southern strategists understood about political power was that they could always use it to control the outcome of any election, as long as the electorate in thirteen key states was controlled. Voting polls were removed from Black and brown neighborhoods, there was voter suppression through draconian voter ID laws, purging voter rolls, and more. There was never real allegiance to any particular party, but instead strategic plays for a specific outcome. The complicity with Russianinterference in recent elections falls against a backdrop of hypocrisy when were member, just a few decades ago, their Red Scare rhetoric and talk of communist threats as to further their —us versus them agenda. This helps us once again understand that the strategy of maintaining the ideology of white supremacy and its dominance was never intended to be challenged. And it definitely was never intended to be replaced.

When I see Mitch McConnell, I see America's past — but not in a modern context. I see an America just after the civil war, when president Andrew Johnson and his peers had the opportunity to banish the crooked lawmakers and laws but failed to do so. The nefarious question is, why? The answer just may be as plain as day: this, too, is inherently American.

McConnell is the epitome of the old South and his refusal to expand Medicaid— along with his GOP colleagues — amounts to slow violence with deadly consequential outcomes. His non-action to resist justice and his method of leadership only appears to be present and carried out with surgical precision when it comes to him stacking the federal courts with 200 judiciary appointees and counting. His commitment to large corporations against a backdrop of stalled tactics to deny those in Kentucky who are less fortunate is even more telling. The problem? McConnell continues to get re-elected.

Southern strategy is more than just a behavior; it is a commitment to a way of life — even if that means one's life will be significantly shortened by policy. We are experiencing history in real time: the policies, outcomes, cultural outlook, and those cumulative impacts in our daily lives. Whether we like the history of it or not, we have been ushered into what Reverend Barber refers to as a third reconstruction period. Initially, when white people heard the words —*Black lives matter," they actually heard, "We are coming to take your whiteness and claim it for ourselves. "Or, perhaps more delicately put, "You are going to force me to share my birthright.*

For a people that were convincingly coerced into buying into the false narrative of color blindness, these words were like nails on a chalkboard. Something that opened my eyes was observing how the mere presence of a few Black and brownfaces in the workplace could become so curious and unsettling for my white coworkers. So very unsettling, in fact, that you would notice how certain people would transfer from that particular department if it got too colorful.

I believe that de jure segregation had been so ingrained in their psyche that it had to play out through this de facto segregationist behavior. Those that were in charge became gatekeepers to stop the fear of this influx of Black and brown faces.

While they did not understand at the time — because, by definition to them, racism simply meant being prejudiced towards another — at the first opportunity they began repopulating this browned workforce with faces from the neighborhood. Because they were so cavalier in their understanding of what justice is supposed to look like, they were withholding opportunity from a broader pool and handing opportunities toa select few [44]. Where they fell short was in lacking the understanding that they were enacting the very tenets of racism. It's prejudice plus power, and policy was added on top of this as rules changed to accomplish their goal.

In the world of the white, male, blue collar worker, it appears that he must abandon the space that renders him vulnerable to change and discomfort, for it requires a certain maturity in order to accept the fact that things change — and the fragility of this construct that is whiteness does not allow for such growth.

One of the tenets of this chapter is the notion that men have to have the ability to destroy in order to preserve their wholeness. Even if that may result in self-harm, the other imperative piece is the violence perpetrated through the willful neglect of others. Both of these constructs are rooted in a mental and moral illness spurred on by the preservation of the false narrative of whiteness.

Though I haven't talked much about guns in this chapter, these realities illuminate the fact that poor decisions are often made by individuals with a warped sense of reality and a gun. I cannot ever recall a time when the consequential outcome was ever good. While it can be suggested that most gun owners are responsible, it should be noted that growing rates of white male suicide by guns is indicative of a larger mental illness issue. This, alongside many other mental and social issues, is derived from violence. To be more specific this is — if we are honest with ourselves — the violence of whiteness. Given the current state of society, what if violence was the intent behind the dogged way that white people refuse to wear masks despite being bombarded with information that Black and brown people are dying at an alarming rate? It falls in line with the white notion that, —Refusal of a national healthcare plan may harm some of us, but it is going to take out more of you. The proverbial you, of course, being more Black folks. This, in my opinion, should be considered cultural warfare, allowing the —silent majority to become quiet soldiers and participate without the bloody heirloom of engaging in the unconscionable act of shooting and maiming.

This is an American issue. Our moral compass becomes skewed when we talk about the perceived need for violence against certain groups. When we do this we often speak of the threat of gang violence coming to a white suburb near you. In reality, these mythical suburbs are fairly safe — and it is because they are not overly scrutinized by the apparatus of an over-militarized police presence.

While it is relevant to speak on, the need for police reform is years overdue. However, it is imperative that we address something that is just as critical of a component to policing: the need to have anti-racist conversations. The former has been approached with an attempt to legislate the antithesis of the latter. Plainly stated, these efforts have failed. We have to understand that we cannot continue to enforce compliance on the front end, when the root cause is an underlying value system based on the idea of a manmade social construct that should have never existed in the first place.

CHAPTER 7

2043 IS COMING AND NOTHING CAN TRUMP THAT

It is a convenient thing to be disillusioned by the intent of those around us when there is no threat to contentment or power. But when we try to forget history, it could only be beneficial to those with power; more succinctly, those with a proclivity towards violence in order to create and maintain that power.

50% of the young people in the country are people of color as of 2020. By 2043, more than 50% of the entire country will be people of color. By the year 2060, multiracial people are projected to more than triple in size from eight million to roughly 27 million in number, perhaps rendering racial labels increasingly irrelevant according to experts [45]. As far as non-Hispanic whites, the news becomes even more alarming, as the number is expected to plateau at 200 million in 2024, and then begin a gradual decline as the generation of Baby Boomers transitions into their golden years.

It has been said that the worst place Black folks can exist is in the imagination of white people. Because of the polarization created through historical de jure segregation, white folks have developed a Black boogeyman, and they become unraveled when the notion of a level playing field for Black folks is even presented. Whiteness is portable, so it has the ability to morph into a phenotype when placed under minor scrutiny — but its most powerful property has to be the ability to conveniently become invisible. No other race on this hierarchical ladder has this ability, so we see how the construct of whiteness will always depend on Black suffering to exist. White America will always face the moral dilemma: will it continue to choose whiteness over democracy?

While this chapter may leave the reader with somewhat of a somber impression, I do not wish to leave the reader with questions about an impending second civil war per se. However, I am also not in the business of selling false hope.

It is my opinion that the moral divide in America is so great that the decay created by centuries of ignored greed and selfishness have become too great an obstacle to overcome. It should be suggested that we wipe the slate clean and begin again. I am uncertain as to what that would look like, so I cannot offer up any hope at this time. I can say that there is nothing new under the sun, and an honest deconstruction of our history is probably our best bet at arriving at some sort of solution. We are at a crossroads that is not too unfamiliar when we reflect upon the words of W. E. B. Du Bois as he prophetically proclaimed that —the problem of the twentieth century is the problem of the color line [46]. And so it is that same question of national identity with which we grapple today.

It is not my hope to reveal a multitude of committed warmongers that are hell bent on driving the country over the edge at the slightest hint of change. It is, however, my desire to reveal a somewhat cult-like cognitive dissonance and the violent nature behind the remnant of a few to undermine the ideology of democracy and citizenship for all. This occurs through a myopic lens of class warfare and racial resentment. One should not be alarmed by this view, but instead be aware that it has always been the impulse of unease displayed historically by white America through bloodshed.

This is almost always the reactionary ritual of choice for safeguarding America as a for-whites-only space. Increased state-sanctioned domestic terrorism alongside of militia guerrilla warfare tactics sounds on par when discussing the particulars. As I observed the behaviors of particular members of this cross-section of men for the better part of thirty years now, I'm convinced that this theory becomes less farfetched with each passing day.

In my experience, I have found that all one had to do was ask some of these folks and they would be more than happy to tell you that they themselves anticipate a race war — but their reasoning was always shortsighted of any personal fears or perceived threats. Others sported a more solemn display of stern silence and the occasional look of paranoia when the break room television was turned on Fox News, as patented dog whistles with racial undertones and overtones would cloud the airwaves. I began to realize that this was not news for them, but more of an escape.

The Fox News channel was often the sounding board of the silent majority, so it was often played nonstop to send out the aforementioned dog whistles to others. Thus, this sentiment is popular — whether or not it jived with company policy.

Talk of reparations legislation, the threat of more stringent mandatory background gun laws, government agency surveillance of domestic terrorism, and galvanized protestors of all colors converge through a media lens to present the image of a vice that is slowly closing its grip on this swath of society soon forcing them out of hidden crevices to reveal them to the world.

And though all of these things seem compelling enough triggers for a major insurrection, the idea that there will be a specific time that no one can combine the two words "white and growth" together will, in my estimation, be the proverbial straw to finally break the camel's back. Swaths of these race soldiers will emerge across America and it will only be a matter of time before Pandora's Box is opened.

The key factor is, as the late Dr. Frances Cress Welsing stated, the need to avoid white genetic annihilation — or at least its optics leading to the year 2043.

Austerity policies and politics have been so cemented in our institutions, past and present, and to such an extent that they have fostered these recurring behaviors and only serve to highlight the fact that our country has always seemed to lean right — even despite popular vote or justifiable critique. What appeared to be left was simply centrism and merely an attempt by our government, through various systems, to hold the right at bay and prevent racial anarchy at all costs. This relationship is often discussed as one represented by two sides with diametrically opposing views. The reality is that it is more of a longstanding symbiotic partnership.

We are forced to also address the fact that this nation not only has a violent past and present, but that the lines between which we teeter are one of civility and one of savagery. In the vein of Dr. Martin Luther King Jr., we must first understand

that violence is also the attitude of indifference towards the suffering of others. It is the intolerance of a shared presence. It is what makes the physical action of killing such a viable option in the eyes of some, and this is what determines the value of certain lives in America and the justification for the plunder of others. It is apparent that the transfer of the fear of a racial overthrow during the civil rights movement of the 1960's has shifted from bureaucrats to the everyday citizenry in fear and distrust of big government, while oligarchs and plutocrats continue to control and shape the narrative of free and unfettered markets. But more importantly, many are trapped into believing that there is no other way. Perhaps they believe that any other way will disrupt the value system that has been created within this centuries-old racial hierarchical system. Therefore, I dare America to be greater than this, and to envision itself as great in totality as it pertains to all of its citizenry.

CHAPTER 8

REPARATIONS NOW

—*Equality is not likely to be obtained without some form of reparations*, avid H. Swinton, an economist and former president of Benedict College, wrote in the 1990 collection The Wealth Of Races. If Black lives matter, then the movement by the same namesake matters [47].

Thus, we must incline our ears to also hear its platform of demands.

While these demands cover critical issues — such as ending the war on Black people, invest-divest, defunding of police departments, economic justice, political power, and community control — one in particular that should be a matter of urgency is reparations.

I dare America to push forth a bill on reparations. Prove to me that this country is not what I believe and have witnessed it to be. Too often, when I look back on the history of this nation, I have seen more injustice as it concerns the red, brown, and Black of this nation than I have seen justice. History has not been favorable to this nation without the aid of spun propaganda, and so it continues to ignore it or piecemeal the few parts that are. As a vested member in its democracy and a child of its promises, I think that it is equitable enough to decry that America must grapple with this portion of its history. On April 16, 1862, President Abraham Lincoln signed the District of Columbia Emancipation Act [48]. This was done with the intention of garnering loyalty to the Union, while easing the pain of those slaveholders who lost property in the form of slaves. The Union awarded a litany of restitutional payments to its former slaveholders to the tune of $300 per freed laborer. Lincoln appointed a board over the process, which reviewed more than 1,000 shareholder petitions. Most of these petitioners received the full amount owed.

If we want to change the way that we are viewed in America, we need to change the way that we are valued in America. The United States was a slave society.

People refer to it as if though it were a bump in the road; it should be contended that slavery *was* the road. Without slavery, the financial system that we have today would not exist. Its expansion westward was literally carved out of the bodies of indigenous people. A system used to machinate its own greed, slavery was capitalism before capitalism was food for fodder. In fact, being a master to the enslaved was seen as societal royalty — just as the celebrities of today have an iconic perception. It was a pinnacled achievement by which the poor of that time could one day hope to achieve.

It should be noted, for those today that are eager to quip that their ancestors did not own slaves, that this reality was due to the fact that those people couldn't afford to own slaves. Thus, they were not heroes, because neither were they abolitionists. People's attitudes were shaped through centuries of that particular institution, and subsequently white supremacy was simply modernized and presented in more palatable forms — such as Jim Crow laws and the continuation of forced second class citizenry, not to mention the present day carceral system. Myself, along with a handful of others, contend that until we have equal protection under the law, we are simply residents — not full-fledged citizens. Until there are substantial compensatory measures, policy, and social change on behalf of America towards its Black citizenry, we are simply residents.

The dehumanization of Black people has been a fundamental part of our history and has been part of American culture for too long. We have seen time and time again that we all come together over brutality at the hands of the police towards unarmed Black men, women, and transgender folks, but that brutality stems from a devaluation of the Black body [49]. When talking about reparations, not only do we mean compensation, but we also need to discuss the transferal of custodial rights of government-sanctioned mistreatment of Black bodies to white citizenry as well as the police.

During the Jim Crow era, as well as the nearly 100 years of affirmative action on behalf of white immigrants via the

Homestead Act and New Deal, white settlers could move westward thanks to the cash and land afforded to them. For Black folks, that wasn't the case. One of the ways that we can get the respect that we deserve — and simultaneously uproot this skin valuation system — is through reparations.

That's right, assigning a monetary and social value to those of us who have identified as Black, African American, etc. and can prove that we have ties to African ancestry dating back to slavery.

In regards to skin valuation I mean specifically the identity with which one associates oneself based on a phenotypic description in order to garner favor, preference, resources, and/or access to spaces otherwise deemed inaccessible to those who do not meet this criteria. To achieve this, we first have to deconstruct the social construct of race.

According to renowned scholar Dr. Jacqueline Battalora, whiteness was established in the English colonies sometime between 1664 and 1681. In 1667, there was a rebellion and probably the most critical insurrection in American history —called Bacon's Rebellion. Because of this year-long rebellion, in 1681 lawmakers created a —divide and conquer strategy that introduced whiteness into law. So, in stark contrast to biological theorists, this creation came along with white privilege and Black and native disenfranchisement.

In 1676, the uprising of a mixed group of mostly indentured and enslaved men that numbered about 1,000, comprised of both Black and white people, waged a revolt against the harsh treatment from the ruling planter class in Virginia and demanded a more even distribution of wealth, power, land, and political inclusion.

The insurrection was unsuccessful, but would become what is known as Bacon's Rebellion. This provided the spark needed to force the ruling class — which was overwhelmingly represented by the elitist class at that time — to establish a set of laws that would create the basis for their perpetual economic dominance and cement their place at the top of the financial hierarchy still seen today. This strategy of —divide and conquer between the poor Anglos and those of African heritage would prove to be a tour de force unlike any other, and would go on to produce an abundance of wealth, waste, and decadence unrivaled in the new world.

The laws were written such that those of European or Anglo descent, regardless of ethnicity, were now given the designation of white. This new possession, called whiteness, would immediately create a buffer class throughout the colonies between the wealthy elite and those designated to a perpetual and permanent economic floor of society. More importantly, it would disunite a growing labor class that overwhelmingly outnumbered the small class of elitists and therefore represented a threat to the social order.

Although, for this newly invented and socially constructed group there was no shared economic power, this designation awarded them the advantage of not being socially ostracized by color, along with certain civil rights: they could now vote and own land, and more importantly, could no longer compete for wages against that part of society that had been removed and reassigned.

The first order of business? The creation of militias, which consisted of the drafting of white men for the task of slave patrol to round up all of the Black potential insurrectionists. Though previously believed to be formed after the establishment of slavery, these groups would always maintain an allegiance to the elites and were dutily responsible for the entrapment of Black bodies and the physical maintenance of a system that would last for the better part of 250 years. This social contract between the rich planters and poor whites, AKA the strategy of —divide and conquer, would coax poor whites into a perpetual state of believing that they were no longer at the bottom of the social ladder. This Faustian bargain for the European indentured servants upon introduction into free society, where they would still be given basic survival tools upon release, now included being armed with whiteness.

This would prove to be a more than effective strategy for the elite class than any other that had been previously devised. Meanwhile, at the same time those unfortunate enough to be deemed Black, regardless of their previous contract of indentured servitude, remained enslaved. Even for those that had been freed, there was the risk of being returned into a system that reduced them to no more than beasts of burden or, as a southern woman of the antebellum south said, —a well-trained pet.

This curse would prove to have devastating consequences that would last well into the 20th century and beyond. As we peel back the first layer of construct, which is race, we must understand that it in itself is a construct built to mask another construct: whiteness. The fascinating thing about the construct of race is that the term is used to neutralize the outward perception of the power of whiteness, and in doing so, it often reduces that perception to a phenotype. It also serves to create a binary of false perception of an equal distribution of power between polar opposites: Black and white. When we understand that this is actually rooted in anti-Blackness and whiteness as power and not phenotype, then whiteness becomes the only central focal point that should be discussed.

Preserving sacred property rights and moving the Negro problem offshore meant that there was no justice for enslaved African Americans. I feel that in the same fashion that plunder occurred in this nation, reparations should be dispersed. In other words, the action should take place and then the justification for that action should occur because otherwise we will waste tons of time trying to explain the wrongs of history. And as such, we will without a doubt be confronted with counter-revolutionary measures to maintain the traditional imbalance of power that we as Americans have grown accustomed to. Justice requires this.

Black people have always been an integral part of capitalism — and not in a good way.

Many European, Asian, and other immigrants came to this country to gain access to resources. They did not need to know the specifics of slavery, just that there was already an economic floor established. They did not need to know that capitalism was and is a predatory system synonymous with the exploitation of those that had been enslaved and those that were the victims of genocide. In fact, I do not know that America could continue to function without the exploitation of the floor class. The problem after ending slavery was finding a suitable system with which to replace it. One that would continue the bloody heirloom of greed and corruption. In 1866, one year after the 13th Amendment was ratified, Alabama, Texas, Louisiana, Arkansas, Georgia, Mississippi, Florida, Tennessee, and South Carolina began to lease out convicts for labor. Called peonage, this made the business of arresting Blacks very lucrative, which is why hundreds of white men were hired by these states as police officers. Their primary responsibility was to search out and arrest Blacks who were in violation of Black Codes. Once arrested, these men, women, and children would be leased to plantations where they would harvest cotton, tobacco, and sugar cane. In other instances, they would be leased to work at coal mines or railroad companies. The owners of these businesses would pay the state for every prisoner who worked for them. And there lies the foundation of prison labor.

The false dichotomy through which the term - race' has been presented is often a linear binary of Black on one side and white on the other, with both sides always struggling to get along. This is purposefully misleading. We should view this structure through the vertical lens through which history teaches us was built on the hierarchy of whiteness. The very essence of it lies in the fact that it is rooted in anti-Blackness. Of course, this was done for the sake of maintaining a power structure that determines who receives access to resources and who is denied access — and this hierarchy still persists. In comparison to other civilizations America is still a young nation, yet she continues to behave in an archaic fashion. It is interesting that white Americans are afraid of what they would lose to Black and brown folks, as opposed to looking through a more global lens at what we would gain. Other westernized nations that have free healthcare for all, stronger schools, less income inequality, etc. have a similarly democratized model and by comparative standards are thriving. We have once again allowed race to put us on the global map for our shortcomings. The Cold War and the Space Race revealed these fissures, but there was not a more damning and detailed report that could have revealed this any more than the Kerner Commission report. The situation of Blacks had been addressed in the Kerner Commission empaneled by President Lyndon Johnson in the aftermath of a number of major urban riots in the late 1960s.

Memorably, the commission concluded that—Our nation is moving toward two societies, one Black, one white — separate and unequal and that—white racism was the cause. The commission recommended massive programs to attack the impoverishment of urban ghettos and improve the well-being of the Black population. But the recommendations got caught in the meat-grinder of presidential politics and Johnson, who had done so much to improve the situation of Blacks up until that point, essentially ignored the findings. Since the Kerner Commission, no such major official effort has been mounted to understand and respond to the inequalities suffered by Black Americans.

The idea of a national commission of inquiry remains crucial to rectifying these long-simmering injustices. Such a commission would help build public support for reparations by analyzing the origins, nature, and causes of racial inequality in the United States. The country's best historians, sociologists, economists, and political scientists would have to be assembled for the job. They would have to look into disparities in health, wages, employment, incarceration, and so much more. Then, on the basis of such an inquiry, appropriate measures could be recommended to Congress. Thus, it was only logical that America continued to invent streams of revenue by way of Black exploitation in avoidance of these great tasks.

For those of us African Americans who grew up in the South, we only had to have a grandmother who endured the harshness of sharecropping during Jim Crow to see the lingering effects of slavery and Jim Crow laws. Picking rows of cotton and peas, nursing the children of others before even getting a chance to encounter their own, and still facing the atrocities that their ancestors faced generations before. They too were indeed dealt a cruel and underserved lifetime of hardship.

Reparations are the only way that you can fix the negative transfer of wealth through free labor, taxation without representation, and sanctioned segregation which together resulted in exclusion from programs that created the white suburban middle class — and virtually shut out the Black community and relegated them to a permanent underclass status. The results of this can be seen today in a 20:1 wealth gap between those that are referred to as white and those who are referred to as Black in America — which was imposed upon Black people over the course of 35 years [50].

A national act of procrastination does not eliminate the debt of reparations. If I were to cut off a man's arm and the arms of those in his family, how long should they wait for justice to be served? 5 days? 5 years? 50 years? In the eyes of those who lost a limb, 50 years is a lifetime of punishment through the lens of not being whole — and worse, not being vindicated. 400 years is a long time and it is not hypothetical.

The labeling system of identity continues to act as a form of enslavement within this settler colonial society. The question often asked by newer immigrants who arrived post-slavery is whether or not they should have to pay reparations. My response is a resounding, —Yes! I'm pretty sure they understand that they didn't arrive in a vacuum society that had no history but was just always a land of promise.

Immigrants were lured to America by the simple fact that, regardless of what you were or were not in your native country, you could come to America for what Tim Wise in his book *White Like Me* refers to as —free stuff, and in the process not be relegated to the already established permanent underclass that is disproportionately overrepresented by its Black people[51]. These immigrants come with a full understanding of how race-based classism works, in particular those who are arriving from Latin and Hispanic countries. Now we see that the recent influx from these groups that identify as Hispanic have injured or damaged the path by which their predecessors have established their identity upon arrival. This is due largely in part to the re-establishment of white identity and the resurgence of white nationalism.

My hope is that there will be a significant push for reparations. So what if people are salty for a generation or two? I want this for that 4th and 5th generation to be grafted into the skin valuation system — or to have it removed once and for all so that we can begin to imagine what an egalitarian society truly looks like. If this isn't feasible, I would love to seize this particular moment in history so that we can unmask white America and reveal that its true intention all along has been to not make us full citizens at all, but to continue to commodify us in order to maintain a 400-year-old system of predatory capitalism and status quo.

CONCLUSION

We are sitting on the proverbial powder keg and no one is talking about it. It has always been the big pink elephant in the room, but no one wants to acknowledge it.

We occupy ourselves with our hyper individualistic lives and we perpetuate the notion that, given time, all things that are wrong in America will magically heal on their own. We live and have operated in a space where smoking mirrors are the norm while truth is just too difficult of a burden to carry. We choose to conveniently ignore it. Those that are designated black in society, do this to avoid confrontation. Those that are assigned whiteness, perhaps to avoid guilt. Either way, both are steeped in cowardice. We fight to protect what we know is wrong, because deep down inside, we know that it is much harder to fight the demons that pave the ways of convenience and comfort. To embrace truth one must somehow be willing to change and yield to a higher standard and America is simply not mature enough to take those steps. I want badly for those that are deeply vested and have devoted to democracy in this nation to keep the faith. In order for that to happen there must be a redistribution of power. While the prophetic words of Frederick Douglas remind us that "power concedes to nothing without a demand" I truly believe that it is this constant demand that is needed in order for America to right its ship and avoid the pitfalls of its empirical ways.

Finally, we must take a long hard look at dismantling the very thing that has been at the crux of oppression in America, greed. If we are to get to that crux, we must peel back the layers that protect it, and in this nation, those lie in the varying degrees of whiteness and class hierarchies. Violence has never resolved conflict, but it certainly has been used to establish ill-gotten narratives that have proven to be unmerited in the end.

BIBLIOGRAPHY

[1] Evan Hill, ―How George Floyd Was Killed in Police Custody - The New York Times, May31, 2020. https://www.nytimes.com/2020/05/31/us/george-floyd-investigation.html.

[2] If superpowers were real: Immortality- Joy Lin TED-Ed. ‖ https://ed.ted.com/lessons/if-superpowers-were-real-immortality-joy-lin.

[3] How can we hold those who benefit from racism accountable? https://www.brookings.edu/blog/the avenue/2018/03/27/how- can-we-hold-those-who-benefit-from-racism-accountable/.

[4] General Santa Anna dies in Mexico City- HISTORY, 1876. https://www.history.com/this-day-in-history/general-santa-anna- dies-in-mexico-city.

[5] House Fly Lifespan: How Long Do They Live? https://www.orkin.com/flies/house-fly/life-expectancy-of-house- fly.

[6] History.com Editors, ―Tulsa Race Massacre-HISTORY. https://www.history.com/topics/roaring-twenties/tulsa-race-massacre.

[7] Carmelita Pickett, ―Rosewood massacre of 1923 | Overview & Facts| Britannica.‖ https://www.britannica.com/topic/Rosewood-riot-of-1923.

[8] The Editors of Encyclopaedia Britannica, —Atlanta Riot of 1906 | Summary, History, & Facts|Britannica. www.britannica.com/event/Atlanta-Riot-of-1906.

[9] ERIC SCHLOSSER, —The Prison-Industrial Complex - The Atlantic. https://www.theatlantic.com/magazine/archive/1998/12/the- prison-industrial-c omplex/304669/

[10] Reverend William J. Barber II, —Rev. William J. Barber II on the Scourge of Environmental Racism ‹Literary Hub, Aug. 25, 2020. https://lithub.com/rev-william-j-barber-ii-on-the-scourge-environmental-racism/

[11] JOSH LEVIN, —The Reagan-Nixon _monkeys' tape, states' rights, and the welfare queen., Aug.01, 2019. https://slate.com/news-and-politics/2019/08/ronald-reagan-richard-nixon-racism-monkeys-tape-jimmy-c arter.html.[12] EVANANDREWS, —How Many U.S. Presidents Owned Enslaved People? -HISTORY, ‖ Sep. 03, 2019. https://www.history.com/news/how-many-u-s-presidents-owned-slaves.

[13] Jefferson' Attitudes Toward Slavery | Thomas Jefferson's Monticello. https://www.monticello.org/thomas-Jefferson/Jefferson-slavery/Jefferson-s-at titudes-toward-slavery/.

[14] The Editors of Encyclopaedia Britannica, —Ronald Reagan | Biography, Facts, & Accomplishments| Britannica. https://www.britannica.com/biography/Ronald-Reagan.

[15] M. Vickerman, ―Recent immigration and race: Continuity and Change, Du Bois Rev., vol. 4, no. 1, pp. 141-165, 2007, doi:10.1017/S1742058X07070087.

[16] Marty Steinberg, ―George HW Bush quotations. https://www.cnbc.com/2018/12/01/george-hw-bush-quotations.html.

[17] STEPHEN M. WALT, ―The Myth of American Exceptionalism - Foreign Policy, ‖ Oct. 11, 2011. https://foreignpolicy.com/2011/10/11/the-myth-of-american-exceptionalism/.

[18] G. Gustavsson, ―The Problem of Individualism Examining the relations between self-reliance, autonomy and civic virtues. ‖

[19] White Guilt: How Blacks and Whites Together Destroyed the Promise of the Civil Rights Era: Steele, Shelby: 9780060578633: Amazon.com: Books, ‖ May 29, 2007. https://www.amazon.com/White-Guilt-Together-Destroyed-Promise/dp/0060578637.

[20] Racial Balance | Encyclopedia.com. ‖ https://www.encyclopedia.com/politics/encyclopedias-almanacs-transcripts-and-maps/racial-balance.

[21] Michael Waldman, ―How the NRA Rewrote the Second Amendment | Brennan Center for Justice, ‖ 2004. https://www.brennancenter.org/our-work/research-reports/how- nra-rewrote-secon d-amendment.

[22]　Casey Michel, ―An Honest History of Texas Begins and Ends With White Supremacy|The New Republic, Mar.12,2021. https://newrepublic.com/article/161685/texas-1836-project-white-supremacy.

[23]　Abraham Lincoln and Emancipation |Articles and Essays |Abraham Lincoln Papers at the Library of Congress | Digital Collections | Library of Congress, Libr. Congr. Washington, D.C. 20540 USA.

[24]　Charleston, ―Fannie Lou Hamer: ‗The flag is drenched with our blood', from ‗The Heritage of Slavery' -1968― Speakola, 1968. https://speakola.com/ideas/fannie-lou-hamer-the-flag-is-drenched-in-blood-1 968.

[25]　R. DiAngelo, ―White Fragility: Why It's So Hard for White People to TalkAbout Racism: DiAngelo, Robin, Dyson, Michael Eric:9780807047415: Amazon.com:Books, 2018. https://www.amazon.com/White-Fragility-People-About-Racism/dp/0807047414.

[26]　B. M. Lane, ―Construction of the Racist Republican, 2014.Accessed: Apr. 04, 2021. [Online]. Available: https://scholarworks.gsu.edu/history_theses/81.

[27]　Are We Headed forAnother Civil War? | BU Today | Boston University. http://www.bu.edu/articles/2019/are-we-headed-for- another-civil-war/.

[28] Gaby Galvin, ―CDC Report: Suicide Rate Up 35% Since 1999 | Healthiest Communities|US News, Apr. 2020. https://www.usnews.com/news/healthiest-communities/articles/2020-04-0 8/cdc-report-suicide-rate-up-35- since-1999.

[29] LAPD officers beat Rodney King on camera - HISTORY.‖ https://www.history.com/this-day-in-history/police-brutality-caught-on-video.

[30] Riots erupt in LosAngeles after police officers are acquitted in Rodney King trial - HISTORY.‖ https://www.history.com/this-day- in-history/riots-erupt-in-los-angeles.

[31] Ranking America's Worst Presidents |Politics| US News.‖ https://www.usnews.com/news/special-reports/the-worst-presidents/articles/ranking-americas-worst-presidents.

[32] Coates, ―We Were Eight Years in Power: An American Tragedy: Coates, Ta-Nehisi:9780399590566: Amazon.com: Books, 2017. https://www.amazon.com/We-Were-Eight-Years- Power/dp/0399590560.

[33] BYRON TAU, ―Obama: _ If I had a son, he'd look like Trayvon' - POLITICO, Mar. 2012. https://www.politico.com/blogs/politico44/2012/03/obama-if-i-had-a-son-hed-loo k-like-trayvon-118439.

[34] The Guardian, ―The gun numbers|Gun crime. https://www.theguardian.com/us-news/2017/nov/15/the-

gun-numbers-just-3-of-a merican-adults-own-a-collective-133m-firearms.

[35] F. C. Mencken and P. Froese, ―Gun Culture in Action, ‖ Soc. Probl., vol. 66, no. 1, pp. 3-27, Feb. 2019, doi: 10.1093/socpro/spx040.

[37] JeremyAdam Smith, ―WhyAre White Men Stockpiling Guns? - Scientific American Blog Network, ‖ Mar.14,2018. https://blogs.scientificamerican.com/observations/why-are-white-men-stockpiling-guns/.

[38] The demographics of gun ownership in the U.S. | Pew Research Center. https://www.pewresearch.org/social-trends/2017/06/22/the-demographics-of-g un-ownership/.

[39] K. O'Brien, W. Forrest, D. Lynott, and M. Daly, ―Racism, Gun Ownership and Gun Control: BiasedAttitudes in US Whites May Policy Decisions,‖ PLoS One, vol.8, no. 10, p. e77552, Oct.2013, doi: 10.1371/journal.pone.0077552.

[40] GUNS, DEMOCRACY, AND THE INSURRECTIONIST IDEA.

[41] wikipedia, ―DyerAnti-lynching Bill, ‖ scalar.usc.edu, Accessed: Apr. 04, 2021. [Online]. Available: http://scalar.usc.edu/nehvectors/stakeman/dyer-anti-lynching-bill.

[42] Ida B. Wells, ―A Red Record, 1895.‖ https://www.digitalhistory.uh.edu/active_learning/exploratio ns/lynching /wells2 .cfm.

[43] President Johnson signs Voting Rights Act - HISTORY.‖ https://www.history.com/this-day-in-history/johnson-signs-voting-rights-act

[44] R.A. Bulatao, N. B. Anderson, and E. and H. in L. L. National Research Council (US) Panel on Race, ―Prejudice and Discrimination, ‖ 2004, [Online]. Available: https://www.ncbi.nlm.nih.gov/books/NBK24680/.

[45] S. L. Colby and J. M. Ortman, ―Population Estimates and Projections Current Population Reports, ‖ 2015. [Online]. Available: www.census.gov.

[46] JeffThomas, ―The Oakland Post. https://oaklandpostonline.com/34148/opinion/the-problem-of-the-twentieth-c entury-is-the-problem-of-the-color-line/.

[47] R. F. (Ed.). America, ―Amazon.com: The Wealth of Races: The Present Value of Benefits from Past Injustices (Contributions in Afro-American &African Studies) (9780313257537): America, Richard F.: Books, ‖ 1990. https://www.amazon.com/Wealth Races-Injustices -Contributions-Afro-American/ dp/0313257531.

[48] H. C.R. Gibbs, ―A Historical Overview of DC Emancipation.‖ https://emancipation.dc.gov/page/historical-overview-dc-emancipation.

[49] K. R. Hairston, ―Dehumanization of the Black American Female: An American/Hawaiian Experience.

[50] THE ASSIMILATION OF AFRO - AMERICANS on JSTOR.‖ https://www.jstor.org/stable/41202827?seq=1.

[51] T. Wise, ―White Like Me: Reflections on Race from a Privileged Son: Wise, Tim: 9781593764258: Amazon.com:Books, 2011. ://www.amazon.com/White-Like-Me-Reflections-Privileged/dp/1593764251.

Made in the USA
Columbia, SC
29 April 2023